RHYTHM & METER PATTERNS
by Gary Chaffee

Contains: Odd Rhythms, Mixed Meters, Metric Modulation, Polyrhythms

THE PATTERNS SERIES

The four books contained in the Patterns series have been designed to help students in developing an awareness of the types of materials currently being used in contemporary drum performance. Throughout the books, many suggestions will be made concerning how these materials can be applied to the drum set. Students should feel free to experiment with these possibilities, as well as any other ideas that they may come up with.

It is important to understand that the books are not sequential and can be worked on in any order. Also, it is not necessary to complete one book before moving on to the next. The various topics that are presented can be worked on in whatever order is the most appropriate for the individual student.

RHYTHM AND METER PATTERNS - Deals with a comprehensive examination of rhythmic and metric materials, including such things as odd-rhythms, polyrhythms, mixed meters, metric modulation and the like.

STICKING PATTERNS - Presents a new approach to stickings with specific emphasis on their application to drum set performance. Also includes materials for accented single strokes, as well as exercises dealing with the use of doubles on the set.

TIME FUNCTIONING PATTERNS - Focuses on time functioning skills in both the jazz and rock areas. Topics include cymbal ostinatos and linear phrasing, as well as melodic and harmonic jazz coordination.

TECHNIQUE PATTERNS - Contains materials that are designed to help students in developing basic technical skills. Includes a wide variety of exercises for the hands, as well as materials for the feet.

© 1976 (Renewed) G C MUSIC
Exclusive Worldwide Distribution by ALFRED PUBLISHING CO., INC.
All Rights Reserved

ABOUT GARY CHAFFEE

Originally from upstate New York, Gary was educated at the State University of New York at Potsdam, (Bachelor of Science, 1966), and DePaul University in Chicago, (Master of Music, 1968).

From 1968 to 1972 Gary was the percussion instructor at Western Illinois University. In 1972 he joined the faculty of the Berklee School of Music in Boston, Massachusetts, and was appointed head of the Percussion Department in 1973.

During his stay at Berklee, Gary was instrumental in developing many new and creative programs for the department, as well as a number of highly successful performance ensembles.

Since leaving Berklee in 1977, Gary has established himself as one of the finest player/teachers in the Boston area. He has performed with many top artists, including Dave Samuels, Pat Metheny, Mick Goodrick, Steve Swallow, Abe Laboriel, Jaco Pastorius, Mike Stern, Bill Frissell, John Abercrombie, Harvey Schwartz and Gary Burton.

From the teaching side, a list of Gary's students reads like a who's who of the contemporary drum scene and includes such people as Vinnie Colaiuta, Steve Smith, Casey Scheurell, Jonathan Mover, David Beal, Joey Kramer and many others.

Gary is also in great demand as a clinician and has performed throughout the United States and Europe. His articles and interviews can be seen in Modern Drummer, Percussioner International, Drum Tracks, Rimshot (Germany), and Rhythm Magazine (England).

TABLE OF CONTENTS

INTRODUCTION 4

GENERAL CONSIDERATIONS
- Hand Position 5
- Motion Principles 7
- Dynamic Considerations 8

PRELIMINARY EXERCISES
- Exercise on Stick Heights 9
- Exercises on Dynamic Switches 10
- Exercise on Gradual Dynamic Shifts 12

SECTION I — RHYTHMIC FIGURES OVER ONE BEAT

RHYTHMIC AND METRIC CONSIDERATIONS 13

> **PART 1 — FIGURES BASED UPON A QUARTER NOTE** 15
>> Exercises on Quarter Note Based Figures 16
>> Studies on Quarter Note Based Figures 18
>>> Studies Involving Rhythmic Mixtures 19
>>> Studies Involving Rests 21
>>> Studies Involving Alternate Notations 30
>>> Studies Involving Partial Subdivision 32
>>> Studies Involving Alternate Rhythmic Placements 34
>>> Study Involving Metric Modulation 35
>
> **PART 2 — FIGURES BASED UPON A DOTTED QUARTER NOTE** 37
>
> **PART 3 — METER STUDIES** 43

SECTION II — RHYTHMIC FIGURES OVER LARGER SPANS OF TIME

> **PART 1 — FIGURES BASED UPON A QUARTER NOTE BEAT UNIT** 55
>> A. Rhythmic Figures Over Two Beats 58
>> B. Rhythmic Figures Over Three Beats 64
>> C. Rhythmic Figures Over Four Beats 72
>
> **PART 2 — FIGURES BASED UPON A DOTTED QUARTER NOTE BEAT UNIT** 79

INTRODUCTION

The materials contained in this text are designed to acquaint students with some of the more contemporary rhythmic and metric devices being used in today's music. Topics that will be dealt with include the use of odd-rhythmic groupings in both quarter note and dotted quarter note meters, polyrhythms over two, three and four beats, mixed meters, metric modulation, as well as other related issues.

The use of such materials first became apparent in the work of certain 20th century composers, including such people as John Cage, Charles Ives, Luciano Berio, Karlheinz Stockhausen and Pierre Boulez. In the last fifteen or twenty years, this same type of material has begun to appear in more popular musical styles, as is evidenced by such groups as Frank Zappa, Weather Report, Don Ellis, The Tony Williams Lifetime and many others.

The reasons for these trends are fairly easy to understand. Western music has historically been concerned primarily with melodic and harmonic issues. It has only been in the last seventy-five years or so that we have begun to take a closer look at this whole issue of musical time. The possibilities in this area are enormous, and it is hoped that this book will help students in beginning to develop some of this potential.

Most of the materials contained in the book are first presented in the form of snare drum pieces. These pieces are designed to acquaint the student with what the materials look and sound like. As you start becoming familiar with them, you should begin experimenting with how they could be used on the set, either in solos or while playing time.

There are some suggestions contained in the book concerning how this could be done. However, you should feel free to work on applying them in whatever way seems the most practical.

Also included in the text is a 'method' of performance which is called the Down-Up Technique. This method deals with an examination of the physical aspects of playing (stroke motions, stick heights, etc.). Such issues constitute what is perhaps the weakest area in the training of young percussionists. The results of this are always easy to see: imbalance between the hands, inability to execute dynamic shifts, problems in switching smoothly and accurately between various stickings, rhythms and the like. The Down-Up Technique offers one means of dealing with such technical considerations and should be carefully studied and practiced.

GENERAL CONSIDERATIONS

Hand Position

Many methods of holding the sticks are currently in use. I would personally recommend the like-hand (matched grip) method. My reasons for this are as follows:

> a. Since both hands use the same position, the student can deal with them on an equal basis, rather than having to approach them as separate entities.
>
> b. Transfer to other percussion instruments is easier since they too use versions of the matched grip.
>
> c. In this position, the wrist can be used in its natural and most powerful turning motion.
>
> d. Since the thumb and first finger are used to hold the stick, the remaining three fingers can be used in the actual playing situation.

In the like-hand method, the wrist normally controls the initial motion of the stick, while the fingers help to regulate various aspects of impact and rebound. In some instances, especially those at lower dynamic levels, the fingers may take over more of the total motion responsibility from the wrists.

The forearm and upper arm are not normally used in most playing situations. However, they should always be kept as loose and relaxed as possible. (The arms are used in those situations where the physical requirements of the instrument demand large motions, as is the case with drum set. In such instances, their job will be to get the hands into playing position.)

In the matched grip, the stick is held between the pad of the thumb and the first joint of the first finger. (This is referred to as the 'fulcrum'.) A space should be visible between the fulcrum fingers. This is done to allow the stick some turning flexibility without necessarily involving the wrist.

The remaining three fingers are placed lightly on the stick, so as to be in a useable position. Also, the stick is not held tightly against the palm, but is positioned slightly away from it. This gives the fingers some room to move the stick.

The butt end of the stick should line up approximately at the center of the wrist line. This allows the wrist to turn in a relatively straight up and down motion, which is by far the easiest and most practical.

Finally, it should be understood that with all the differences in hand size, stick weight and length, etc., one can and should expect variations from individual to individual in these holding procedures. There are, in fact, many different versions of the matched grip, and the student may find it helpful to experiment with a number of different possibilities.

DEDICATION

"To Carol and Bridgett, for putting up with 20 years of 'pounding' and for always being supportive."

Motion Principles — The Down-Up Technique

The materials contained in this text demand a high degree of facility and control. In order to develop such skills, it is necessary for the student to understand how the hands are used in various performance situations. This is the main purpose of the Down-Up Technique.

The Down-Up Technique is a method by which the student can learn 'how' to play. It consists essentially of two components: Stick Heights and Stroke Types.

Stick Heights — The sticks can be used in any number of height positions off the drum from low (15°) to high (90°). Because of the effects of height on impact, these positions can be related to dynamic levels.

height —	90°	75°	60°	45°	30°	15°
dynamic —	*ff*	*f*	*mf*	*mp*	*p*	*pp*

Stroke Types — In any given dynamic situation, the sticks will normally start and end in the same relative height position. This type of stroke will be referred to in terms of its size (i.e. a 45° stroke, a 60° stroke, etc.).

motion —						
height/dynamic	90°-*ff*	75°-*f*	60°-*mf*	45°-*mp*	30°-*p*	15°-*pp*

It should be understood that the downward and upward motions are not separated, but are rather parts of a continuous process. The entire stroke should be executed as quickly as possible.

There are two reasons why this type of motion procedure is necessary. First of all, on most percussion instruments, once the surface has been struck, it should be allowed to vibrate freely. Secondly, by completing the motion as soon as possible, the student will be preparing for upcoming strokes and will avoid any time loss in this respect.

Dynamic Considerations

In situations involving dynamic mixtures, the sticks are obviously going to have to make adjustments between the various heights. These adjustments can be executed through the use of two additional stroke types.

Up Stroke ↓| Starts in a lower position and moves to a higher position after impact.

Down Stroke ↓↑ Starts in a higher position and moves to a lower position after impact.

The Up Stroke is used when moving to a higher dynamic level, while the Down Stroke is used when moving to the lower levels.

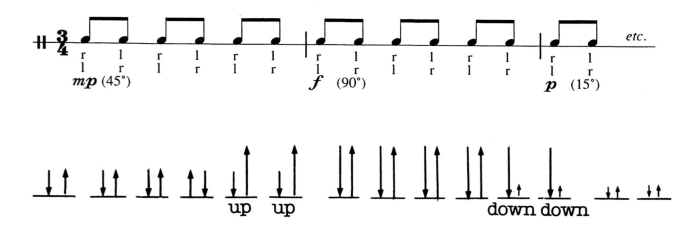

These motion principles will serve as the basis upon which the student can begin to develop a degree of dynamic control. Generally speaking, the principles that have been discussed relate primarily to single strokes, which are used almost exclusively throughout this text. Additional motion possibilities as related to other types of stickings will be dealt with in the book STICKING PATTERNS.

PRELIMINARY EXERCISES

The exercises that follow deal with the hand position and motion principles that have been discussed. Each should be carefully studied and practiced.

EXERCISE ON STICK HEIGHTS

This exercise is designed to help develop an initial degree of control at each of the various stick heights. In each succeeding measure, a different dynamic is used. Therefore, the sticks will have to change heights when moving between the measures. These changes will be made by using the Up and Down strokes.

The exercise should be repeated many times, first with one hand, then the other. Do not try to play it too fast. Rather, concentrate on the stick heights, moving between them as smoothly and as accurately as possible.

All turning motions are made through a combination of finger and wrist usage. At the lower levels, the fingers may take over more of the total motion responsibility.

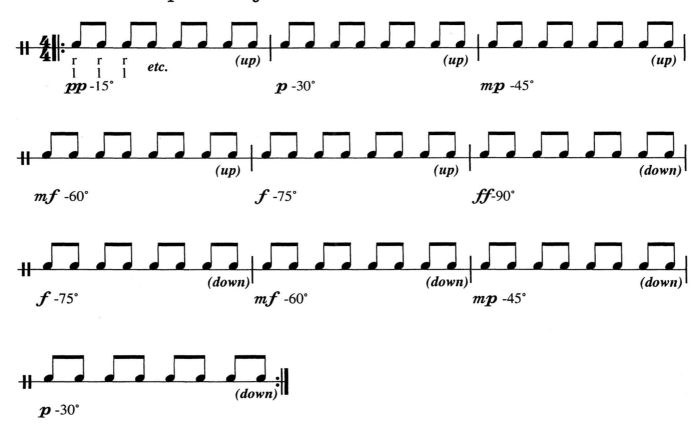

EXERCISES ON DYNAMIC SWITCHES
(Alternating Single Strokes)

Each of the following exercises deals with a different combination of dynamics. When performing the exercises, make sure that the correct height relationships are being maintained in the hands.

Each exercise should be repeated many times, starting with either hand. (Use alternating single strokes.) Work at a variety of tempos, ranging from slow to fast.

(Note: u and d refer respectively to Up and Down strokes.)

1.

  r l r l etc.
  l r l r
  pp (15°)   *p* (30°)
                     u u   d d

2.

  pp (15°)   *mp* (45°)
                     u u   d d

3.

  pp (15°)   *mf* (60°)
                     u u   d d

4.

  pp (15°)   *f* (75°)
                     u u   d d

5.

  pp (15°)   *ff* (90°)
                     u u   d d

6.

  p (30°)   *mp* (45°)
                     u u   d d

EXERCISE ON GRADUAL DYNAMIC SHIFTS

In the previous exercises, abrupt changes were made between the various dynamic levels. Through the use of crescendos and diminuendos, it is possible to have shifts that are more gradual in nature. The exercise that follows deals with these devices.

Repeat the exercise many times, starting with either hand. (Use alternating single strokes.) Work at a variety of tempos, ranging from slow to fast.

When performing the exercise, the dynamic shifts should be executed as smoothly as possible. In doing so, you will actually be using a number of gradations between the six main heights.

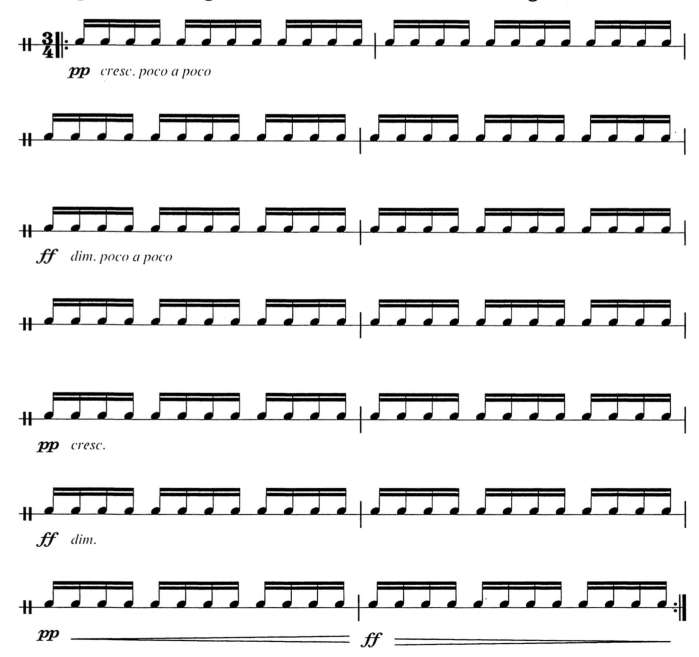

SECTION I

RHYTHMIC FIGURES OVER ONE BEAT

Rhythmic Considerations

A wide variety of rhythms have been used in Section I. Such figures can be counted in any number of ways, as in the following examples:

Numbers **Numbers & Syllables** **One Syllable**

♪♪ ♪♪♪ ♪♪♪♪   ♪♪ ♪♪♪ ♪♪♪♪   ♪♪ ♪♪♪ ♪♪♪♪

1 2   1 2 3   1 2 3 4   1 &   1 & ah   1 e & ah   Da Da   Da Da Da   Da Da Da Da

Each of these systems has advantages as well as disadvantages. For example, the numbers seem to be fairly clear, since they refer specifically to the grouping being performed. They indicate the number of notes in the grouping, as well as the relative position of each note (i.e. two always refers to the 2nd note, etc.). However, the numbers may be somewhat difficult to pronounce at rapid tempos, which is one of the reasons why syllables are sometimes used. Also, many people find it easier to deal with the issue of duration by saying a sound rather than a number. For example:

Da Da Da Da__ Da__ Da__

The student may find it helpful to use some of these counting procedures when initially approaching various rhythmic groupings and combinations. However, it should be understood that the use of such procedures in no way assures the correct performance of a given musical phrase. This is much more the result of physical control and aural perception, and so it is to these issues that the greatest amount of attention should be directed.

Metric Considerations

Musical events exist in some spectrum of time. One of the ways to organize these events is through meter signatures. Basically speaking, meters act as a kind of framework into which the events are placed. Our perception of a given metric situation is inherently dependent upon a number of interrelated factors, including such things as the rhythmic events being used, the ways in which these events are being phrased, the tempo at which the events are being performed, and the actual (or implied) stresses that are present. Therefore, when approaching a given meter or group of meters, each of these issues must be carefully considered.

Beat And Pulse

The terms beat and pulse are often used in association with meter. For the purposes of this text, beat will refer to the mathematical unit (note value) around which the figures are being organized. Pulse, on the other hand, has to do with the shaping of the various events in the overall time scheme. The pulse may be regular, in which case it will often be aligned to some degree with the beat value. However, through the use of meter switches and/or complexities in the rhythmic figures being used, it is possible to have a pulse that is quite irregular and in some cases will be nonexistent.

Foot Tapping

I would strongly suggest that foot tapping be avoided as much as possible. At best, foot tapping is a tool of limited value and at times may actually impede the success with which musical events are realized.

If you wish to check the steadiness of your time, use a metronome. However, the real goal is the development of a highly internalized sense of time; that is to say, time that needs no external reinforcements outside of the music itself.

Part 1 — Figures Based Upon A Quarter Note

A quarter note can be naturally subdivided into the following:

In addition, other numerical subdivisions of the quarter note are also possible:

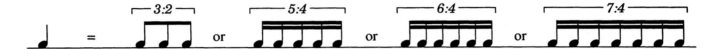

These bracketed figures are sometimes referred to as 'artificial' groupings. In each of these figures, two numerals are present. The first refers to the number of notes in the grouping, while the second indicates the amount of time allotted for these notes. Thus, in the case of the 3:2 figure (which is commonly known as an eighth note triplet), three eighth notes are played in the same amount of time normally allotted to two eighths. The remaining figures are interpreted in a similar fashion:

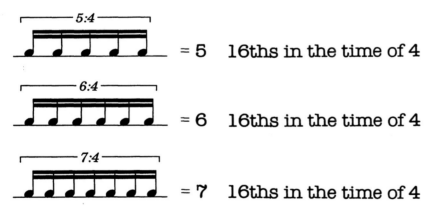

Some composers notate artificial rhythms with one numeral rather than two.

In certain cases, this might be enough. However, I personally favor the use of two numbers, since they supply more basic information. This is especially true in regards to larger rhythmic figures, as will be seen in Section II of this text.

EXERCISES ON QUARTER NOTE BASED FIGURES

The following exercises deal with various combinations of quarter note based figures. Each exercise should be repeated many times, starting with either hand. (Use alternating single strokes.)

When initially practicing the exercises, I would suggest using a moderate stick height (around 45°). Once this has been done, review each exercise at the remaining heights until you feel comfortable performing the figures in any dynamic situation.

♩ = 60-96

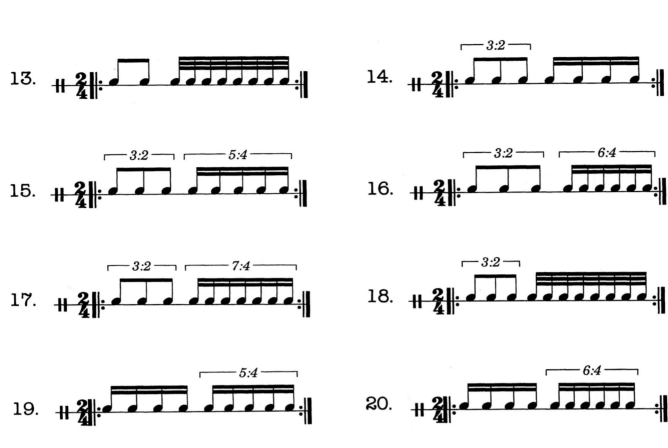

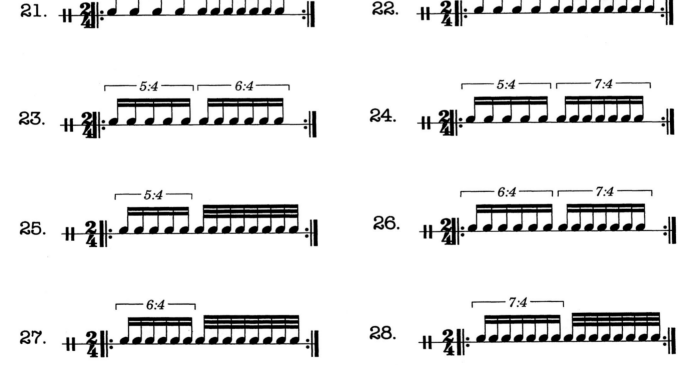

STUDIES ON QUARTER NOTE BASED FIGURES

The following studies use quarter note based figures in a wide variety of situations. When initially working on a given study, it may prove helpful to omit the indicated dynamics in order to concentrate more fully on the placement of the events. Later, the studies should be practiced with the dynamics. When doing so, be constantly aware of maintaining the correct height relationships between the hands.

All tempo indications are relative. The studies may be practiced much slower (or faster) than indicated.

Suggestions For Drum Set Performance — After performing the studies on snare drum, experiment with applying them to the drum set. What events are played will be determined by the particular piece. However, the placement of these events on the set will be improvised by the student.

When initially attempting this, it might be a good idea to set up some fairly simple and specific routines. (For example, you could play an entire study between the snare drum and small tom-tom, switching from one instrument to the other at the beginning of each succeeding measure.) Gradually, however, your routines should become very open and changeable until they are almost totally spontaneous.

Many of these pieces (especially those involving only one meter) can be performed while sustaining various foot ostinatos. Some basic possibilities are:

Studies Involving Rhythmic Mixtures

Study #1. ♩ = 96

Study #2. A variety of quarter note meters are used in this study.

♩ = 96

Studies Involving Rests

Study #3. Two note rhythm with rests.

♩ = 208

Study #4. Three note rhythm with rests.

♩ = 160

Study #5. Four note rhythm with rests.

♩ = 152

Study #6. Five note rhythm with rests.

♩ = 112

Study #7. Six note rhythm with rests.

Study #8. Seven note rhythm with rests.

♩ = 88

Study #9. Eight note rhythm with rests.

♩ = 84

27

Study #10. Rhythmic mixtures with rests.

Study #11. Rhythmic mixtures with rests. A variety of quarter note meters are used in this study.

Studies Involving Alternate Notations

Study #12. Up to this point, the various rests within a given figure have been individually notated. In this study, certain groupings of rests will be combined.

Other figures will be notated in a similar fashion.

Study #13. This study deals with another type of notational alteration.

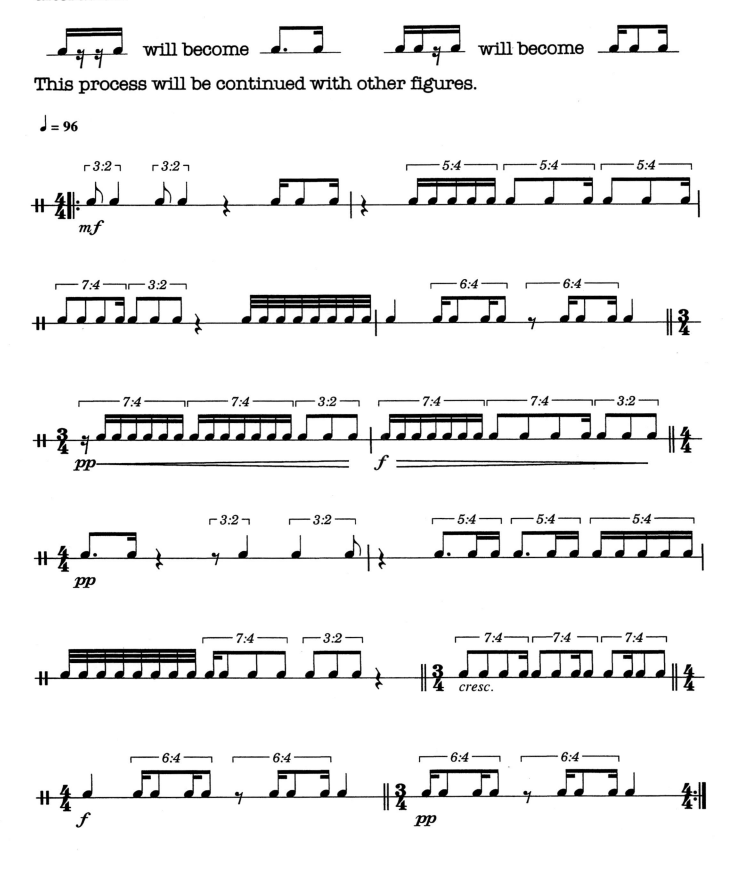

Studies Involving Partial Subdivision

The individual partials of any given figure can be subdivided in a variety of ways. For example:

In this example, certain sixteenth-note partials were subdivided into two, then three parts.

The two studies that follow deal with some of the basic possibilities related to the use of partial subdivisions.

Study #14.

Study #15.

♩ = 80

Study Involving Alternate Rhythmic Placements

Study #16. In this study, some of the rhythmic figures are placed at alternate points within the measure. These should be carefully noted and executed.

♩ = 100

Study Involving Metric Modulation

The term metric modulation refers to a process that can be used to alter the relationships between various rhythms and meters. For example:

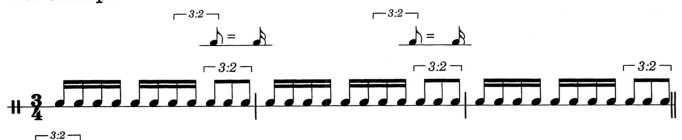

The ♪ = ♪ notation between the first two measures indicates that the speed of the eighth notes in the triplet will become the new speed for the sixteenth notes in the second measure. In like fashion, the speed of the eighth note triplet in the second measure becomes the new speed for the sixteenth notes in the third measure. Therefore, each measure, although identical in notation, will move at a slower speed.

You can also have situations in which the speed of events will increase.

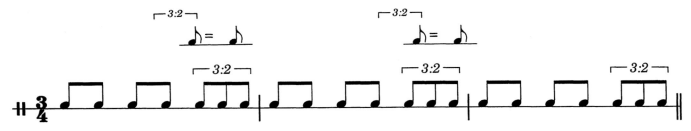

By mixing these procedures, a wide variety of shifts and changes in the rhythmic flow can be created.

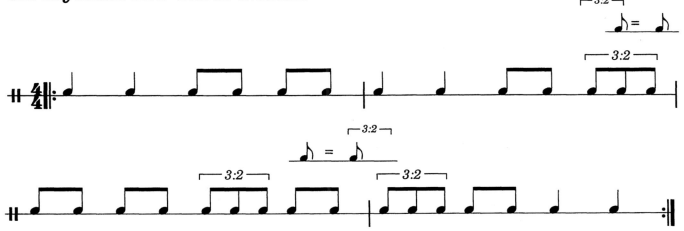

The study that follows deals with some of these possibilities.

Study #17. The starting (and ending) tempo for this study is:

♩ = 84

Part 2 — Figures Based Upon A Dotted Quarter Note

The kinds of rhythmic figures that were dealt with in terms of a quarter note can be constructed using other note values. The graph that follows indicates some of the possible notations for such figures in relationship to a dotted quarter note.

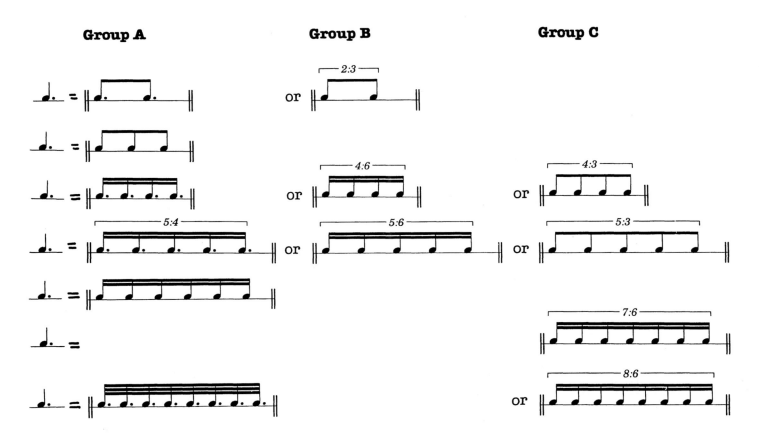

For the two, four, five and eight note groupings, a number of notational possibilities exist. In Group A, these figures are written using smaller dotted note values, thereby eliminating in most cases the need for brackets. In Group B, the reference is made *ahead* to the next natural grouping of notes. (For example, in the 2:3 figure, the three refers to a grouping of three eighth notes.) With Group C, the reference is made *back* to the last natural grouping of notes, as was the case with quarter note based figures.

There are two main reasons why these alternate notational possibilities need to be dealt with. The first has to do with the fact that all are presently in use by composers. No single system has yet predominated, so the student should be familiar with each of them, especially from a reading standpoint. Secondly, all of these alternate notations can be used as a means of developing certain rhythmic structures over larger spans of time. (This point will become more evident in Section II of this text.)

The set of studies that follows will give the student some preliminary practice in dealing with rhythmic figures based upon a dotted quarter note.

Study #18. In this study, the two, four, five and eight note groupings are written using dotted note values.

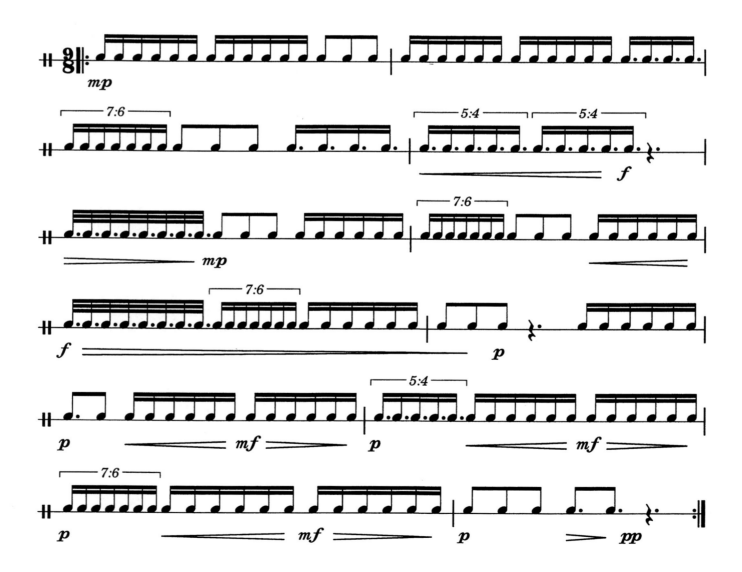

Study #19. Dotted quarter note based figures with rests. Group B notations are used in this study.

♩. = 88

Study #20. Group C notations are used in this study.

♩. = 92

Study #21. Dotted quarter note based figures employing partial subdivision.

Study #22. Dotted quarter note based figures with metric modulation. The starting (and ending) tempo for this study is:

♩. = 80

Part 3 — Meter Studies

The studies that follow deal with some additional metric possibilities and should be carefully practiced.

Meters In 'One'
Certain meter signatures will sometimes be used in 'one', meaning that they are to be thought of with one beat unit per measure. (This is most common with odd numerical meters, such as three, five and seven.) By using such a process, it is possible to create some interesting shapes. As an example of this, consider the following:

M.M. ♩. = 76

The four sixteenth notes in the first two measures are replaced respectively by five sixteenth notes and an eighth note triplet in the third and fourth measures, and each of these figures exists over only two-thirds of a beat unit.

Studies #23-25 deal with this type of situation.

Study #23. 3/8 in 'one'. A dotted quarter note is the beat unit.

♩. = 84

Study #24. 5/16 in 'one'. Note carefully the triplet subdivisions beginning in measure 21.

Study #25. 7/16 in 'one'. Note carefully the distribution between measures 13 and 14.

Meter Subdivision — Meter Combination

Up to this point, all of the metric situations have involved an even (constant) beat structure. In many instances, meters can be used to develop an uneven beat structure. For example:

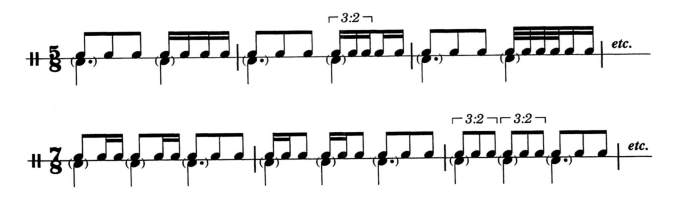

In the 5/8 example, the rhythms have been organized in terms of a dotted quarter note-quarter note beat structure. In the 7/8 example, the implied beat structure is quarter note-quarter note-dotted quarter note. This is what is meant by 'meter subdivision'.

Another way of achieving an uneven beat structure is to mix various meters as in the following example:

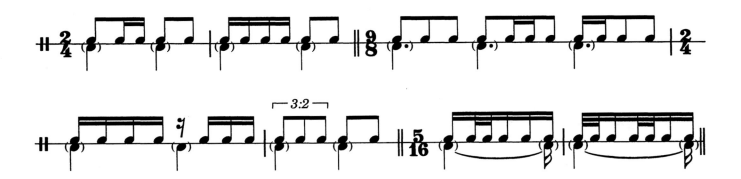

The group of studies that follows deals with these two processes and should be carefully studied and practiced.

Study #26. 5/8 in a subdivision of three-to-two.

One measure of 5/8 ♩. ♩ ‖ = 42

Study #27. 7/8 in a subdivision of two-two-three.

One measure of 7/8 ♩ ♩ ♩. ‖ = 42

Study #28. 11/16 in a subdivision of four-four-three.

Study #29. In this study, quarter note and dotted quarter note beat units have been mixed. The opening tempo is:

♩ = 132

Study #30. Some additional rhythms are used in this study. The opening tempo is:

♩ = 96

Study #31. A variety of meters are used in this study. The opening tempo is:

♩ = 100

Study #32. The final study in this section is 'a-metric', meaning that no meter indications have been given. The opening tempo is:

$\quarternote = 80$

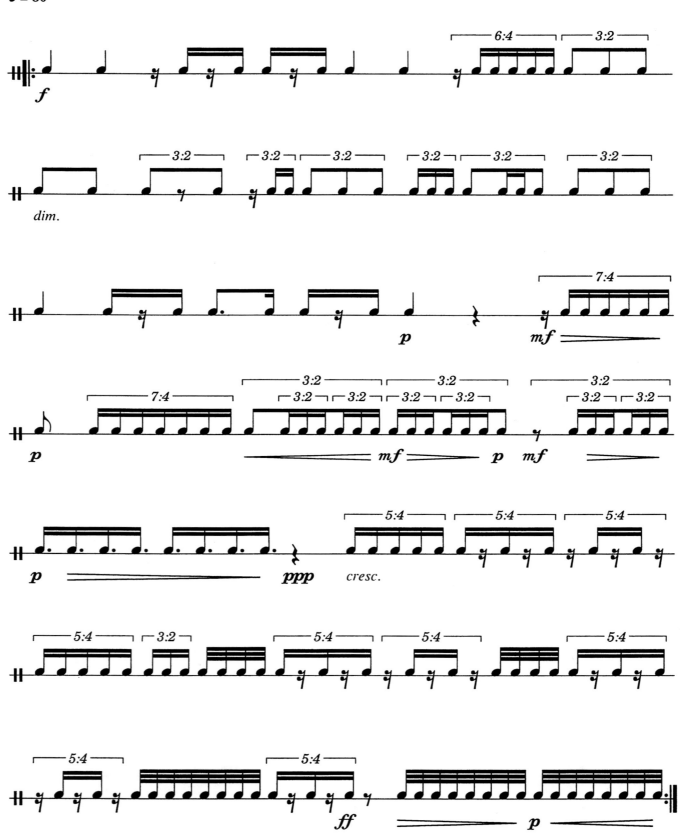

SECTION II — RHYTHMIC FIGURES OVER LARGER SPANS OF TIME

Part 1 — Figures Based Upon A Quarter Note Beat Unit

The kinds of rhythmic figures that were introduced in Section I can be used as a means of creating similar structures over larger spans of time. Basically, this is accomplished by playing only certain partials of a given group. This process will be referred to as 'partial elimination'. As an example of this, by sounding every other note in a series of eighth note triplets, a quarter note triplet is created.

In like fashion, by sounding only every fourth note in the series, a half note triplet is formed.

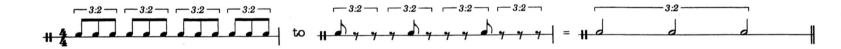

This kind of approach offers a fairly simple means of initially learning how to play the larger rhythmic structures. However, it should not be thought of as a final process. There are two important reasons for this:

1. At extremely fast tempos, it would obviously be impossible to think of (count) all of the smaller partials within a given rhythmic structure, and

2. Even in those tempo ranges where it would be possible, the continued use of such a counting procedure would tend to make the time feel extremely rigid, having little, if any, shape or direction.

The process of using smaller figures to create larger ones is merely a first step. Eventually, the larger structures will have to be considered in and of themselves. The exercises and studies that follow will aid in the development of this skill. They have been divided into three groups:

    A. Rhythmic Figures Over Two Beats
    B. Rhythmic Figures Over Three Beats
    C. Rhythmic Figures Over Four Beats

For each group, two types of exercises will precede the studies. They are preliminary and mixture exercises.

Preliminary Exercises

Each of these exercises will be divided into three measures, as in the following example:

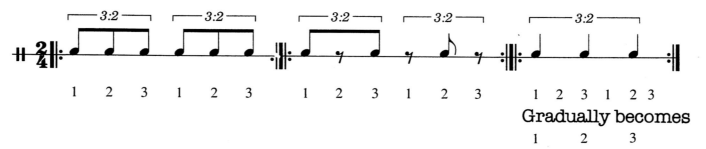

The first measure shows the basic single beat figure that will be used to develop the larger structure. In the second measure, this figure is used with certain partials eliminated. The larger structure created by this process is then shown in the third measure. Practice procedure for the exercise is as follows:

a. The first measure should be repeated a number of times in order to establish the basic rhythmic flow. Once this has been done, move directly into the second measure with no pause.

b. When performing the second measure, you should still be thinking in terms of all the partials including those not being sounded. (This is what the numbers underneath the notes represent.)

c. Next, a move is made into the third measure. On the first few repetitions, continue thinking as you were in the first and second measures. Gradually, however, you should begin to consider the larger grouping as a separate entity without the underlying subdivisions. (This is what the second set of numbers underneath the third measure refers to.)

What we are striving for is the ability to perceive the larger groupings individually without the need for further subdivisions. The first few times you attempt this, it may prove to be a bit shaky, which is to be expected. However, in time, these larger figures should become as natural and comfortable as similar figures over a single beat.

(Note - It should be understood that the numbers used in the previous example merely indicate the kind of thinking process being used. They do not necessarily represent what one would actually count, if anything at all, in such a situation.)

Mixture Exercises

In the mixture exercises, the larger rhythmic groupings are combined into a continuous phrase.

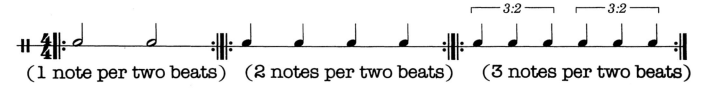

(1 note per two beats) (2 notes per two beats) (3 notes per two beats)

When initially practicing the exercise, each measure can be repeated a number of times. As a given measure becomes comfortable, move directly to the next with no pause.

After performing the exercise in this fashion, one particular alternative is suggested. Rather than moving successively through the measures, practice making more random switches; (i.e. measure 2 to measure 7 to measure 4, etc.). When using this procedure, you should vary not only the order of the measures, but also the number of repetitions for each.

Both types of exercises should be practiced at a variety of tempos and dynamic levels.

A. RHYTHMIC FIGURES OVER TWO BEATS.

Preliminary Exercises

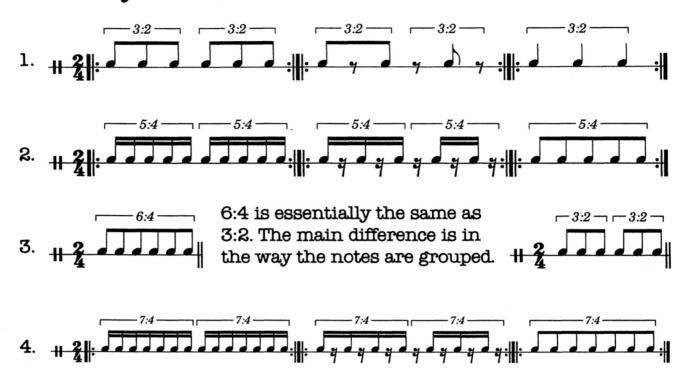

Exercise On Rhythmic Mixtures

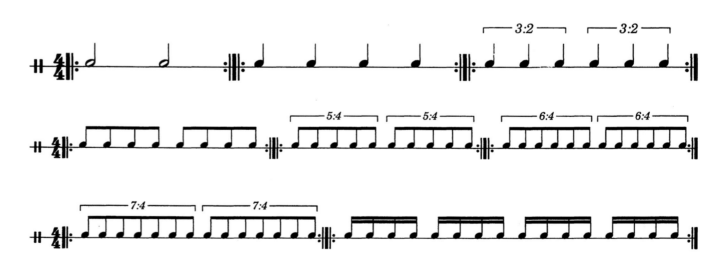

Study #1. Mixtures of Rhythmic Groupings.

59

Study #2. In this study, one and two beat figures are mixed.

♩ = 176

Study #3. The mixtures in this study are more varied.

♩ = 96

Figures Over Two Beats Between The Hands

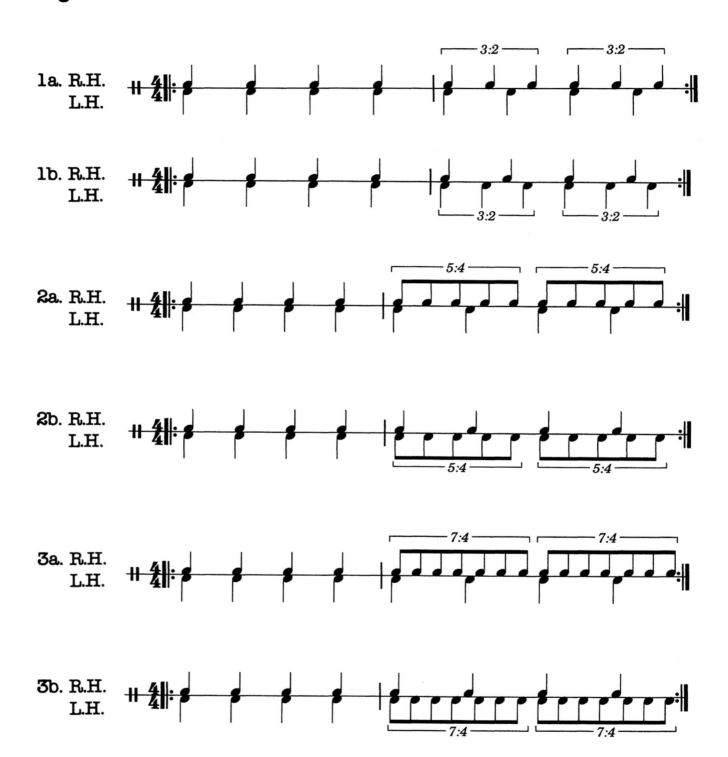

These exercises can also be practiced between a hand and a foot, or both feet.

Study #4. Duet for one player. In this study, an ostinato is sustained in the lower voice while the upper voice plays a variety of rhythms. Initially the study can be performed on two snare drums. Later, experiment with other instrument combinations.

♩ = 126

B. FIGURES OVER THREE BEATS

Preliminary Exercises

1.

2.

3.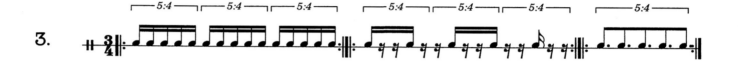

4.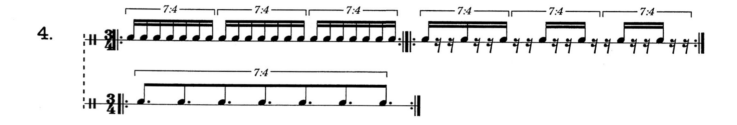

5.

In the preceding examples, the larger figures were written using dotted note values. Although these notations are mathematically correct, such figures are often written in other ways.

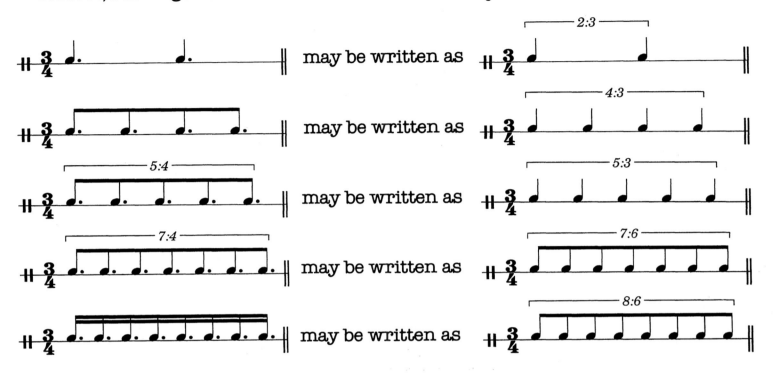

Both types of notations have been used in the studies.

Exercise On Rhythmic Mixtures

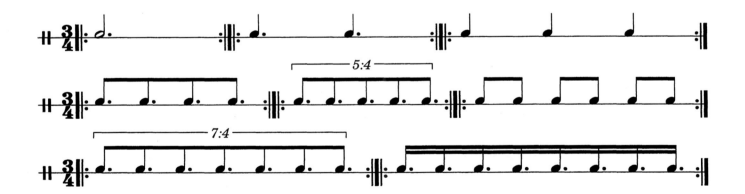

Study #5.

♩ = 184

Study #6. In this study, the larger rhythmic groupings are written using alternate notations.

♩ = 160

Study #7. Figures over one, two and three beats are mixed in this study.

♩ = 120

Study #8. Some meter switches are used in this study.

♩ = 112

Figures Over Three Beats Between The Hands

Study #9. Duet for one player.

♩ = 120

71

C. FIGURES OVER FOUR BEATS

Preliminary Exercises

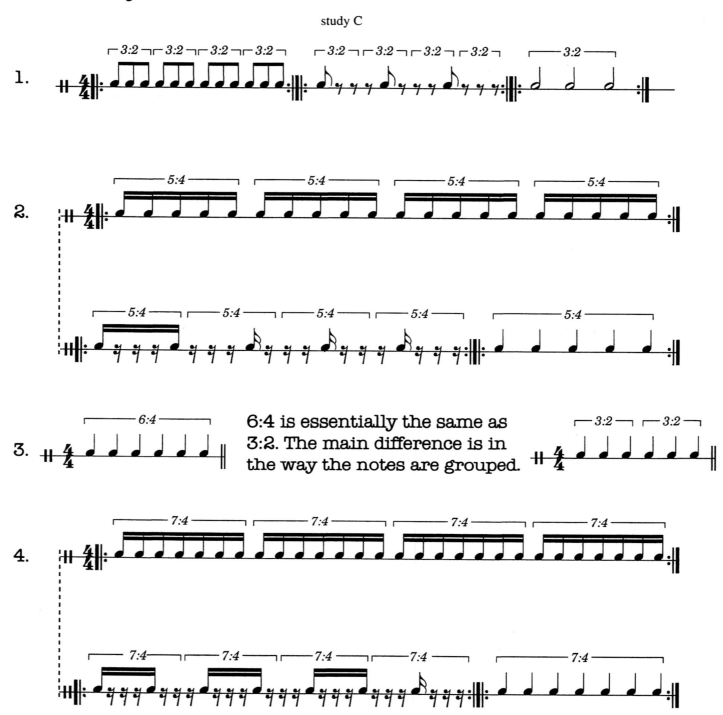

6:4 is essentially the same as 3:2. The main difference is in the way the notes are grouped.

In the examples above, figures over one beat were used as a basis for creating the four-beat structures. An alternative to this would be to use figures over two beats, as in the following exercises.

Exercise On Rhythmic Mixtures

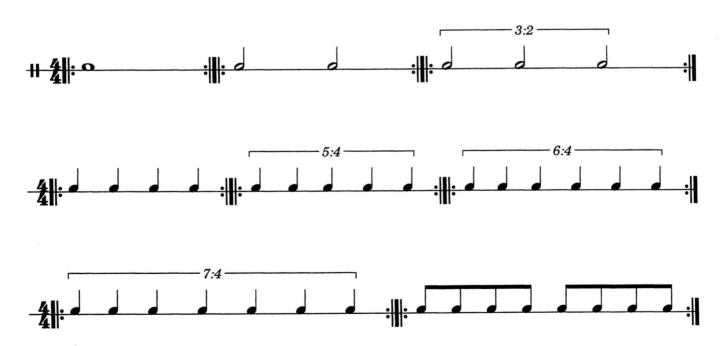

Study #10.

♩ = 120

Study #11. Mixtures of one, two, three and four beat figures. Note carefully the rhythmic distribution in the seventh line.

♩ = 96

Study #12. Some meter switches are used in this study.

♩ = 104

Figures Over Four Beats Between The Hands

Study #13. Duet for one player.

♩ = 132

78

Part 2 — Figures Based Upon A Dotted Quarter Note Beat Unit

The materials that follow deal with rhythmic figures over larger spans of time in relationship to a dotted quarter note beat unit. Our primary concern will be that of notation, since the performance aspects related to such figures have already been covered in Part 1.

Combination Exercises

Figures Over Two Beats

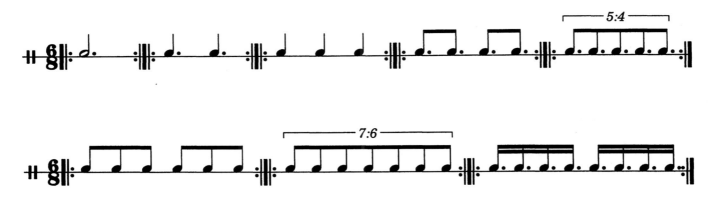

In some instances, the four, five and eight note groupings will be written using alternate notational forms, as in the following examples:

Figures Over Three Beats

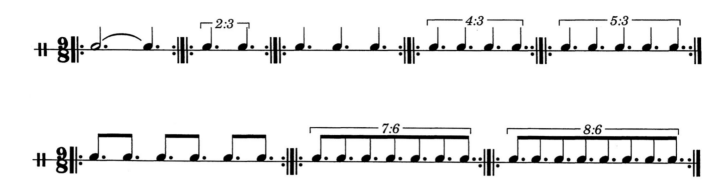

In some instances, the seven and eight note groupings will be written as follows:

Figures Over Four Beats

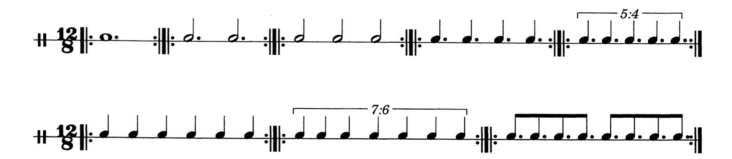

The seven note grouping may be written as follows:

Study #14. The rhythms in this study are derived from three note groupings over one, two and four beats.

♩. = 144

Study #15. This study deals with two, four and eight note rhythmic groupings over three beats.

♩. = 138

Study #16. This study deals with the use of five note groupings over two, three and four beats.

♩. = 152

Study #17. This study deals with the use of seven note groupings over two, three and four beats.

♩. = 144

Study #18. Rhythmic mixtures.

85

Study #19. Rhythmic mixtures. A variety of meters are used in this study.

♩. = 132